FIND OUT ABOUT

Clay

This edition 2002

© Franklin Watts 1994

Franklin Watts
96 Leonard Street
LONDON EC2A 4XD

Franklin Watts Australia
45-51 Huntley Street
Alexandria
NSW 2015

ISBN: 0 7496 4774 4

Dewey Decimal Classification 553.6

A CIP catalogue record for this book
is available from the British Library

Editor: Annabel Martin
Design: Thumb Design
Cover Design: Chloe Cheesman

Additional photographs: © J. Allan Cash 28;
Robert Harding Picture Library 29;
Michael Holford 13, 14, 15, 27; The Hutchison
Library 26; NASA/Genesis Space Photo Library 31.

Printed in Hong Kong, China

FIND OUT ABOUT
Clay

Henry Pluckrose
Photography by Chris Fairclough

FRANKLIN WATTS
LONDON • SYDNEY

This is a lump of clay.
It has been dug
from the earth.

When clay is in the earth
it is often wet and sticky.
It looks just like thick mud.

Before it can be used,
clay must be cleaned.
A potter must have clay
which is smooth and solid.

The clean clay is then ready to be sold. There are different types of clay which potters can buy.

Damp clay is soft and easy to mould.
A potter can use a wheel
to make things from clay.

As the wheel turns
the potter forms the lump of clay
into a pot, a mug or a jug.

When the clay model or pot
has dried it is
baked or "fired" in a kiln.
A kiln is like an oven.
It is heated by gas or electricity.
The heat makes the clay go hard.

When the kiln has cooled the objects are taken out and decorated. Some may be painted before they are given a coat of glaze.

Some are just dipped in glaze.
A glaze is made from
special chemicals.
The glaze sticks
onto the clay surface.

When the glaze has dried
the pots and models
are fired again.
The heat inside the kiln
melts the glaze.
Things made of glazed clay
have a smooth, shiny surface.

When they have been fired
things made from clay
are very strong.
They can be broken –
but the pieces will not rot.
Things made of clay
help scientists and historians
learn how people lived long ago.
The early people of Sumeria
wrote on clay tablets.

We can learn about the Ancient Greeks by looking at the pictures on their pots.

Because fired clay
is so tough it is used
in many different ways.

Bricks are made of clay.
The clay is shaped into bricks.
These are then fired in
a very large kiln.

Walls made of brick are strong.
Brick walls keep the inside
of the house dry.
They will help to keep
the house warm in winter
and cool in summer.

Things made of clay
are used in many other
parts of the house.
Roof tiles are often made of clay.
Why do you think they overlap?

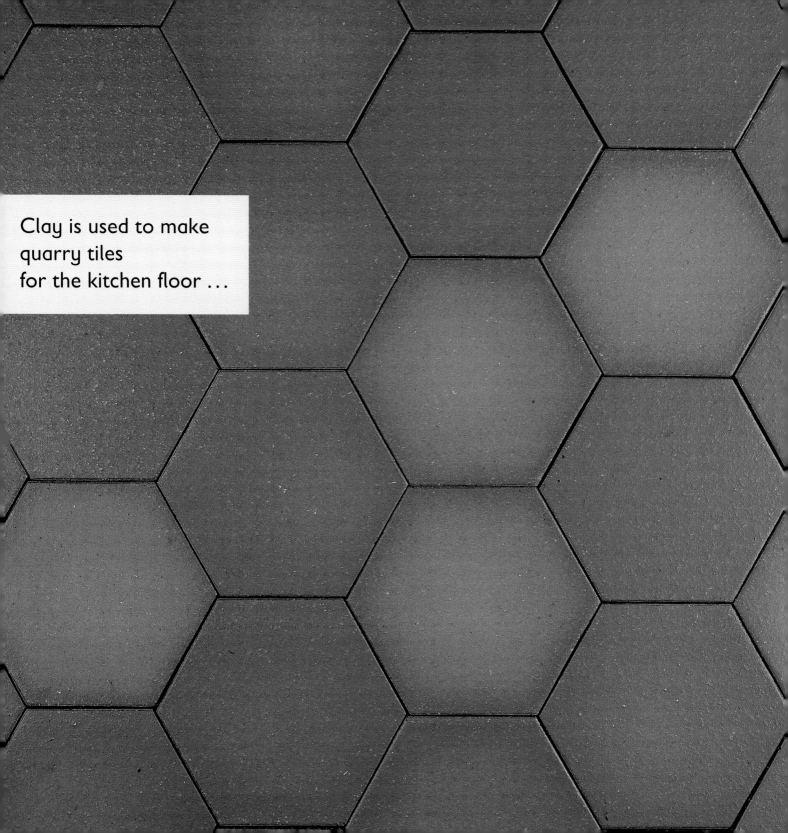

Clay is used to make
quarry tiles
for the kitchen floor ...

and decorated tiles
for the bathroom
and the kitchen.

We use clay to make pipes and chimney pots ...

flower pots
and garden ornaments.

In our homes we have
many things which
have been made from clay —
pots, plates, vases and teapots,
jugs, dishes and mugs ...

as well as ornaments.

People all around the world use clay to make models.

This model was made
by a Greek potter who lived
3000 years ago.

Clay is found
in several colours.
Many years ago
white clay was used
by the Chinese
to make a special
kind of pottery
called porcelain.
Porcelain is so thin
that you can almost
see through it.

Porcelain is made in Europe as well. White clay is mixed with the powdered bones of animals. Cups and saucers made like this are called "bone china." Can you think why?

Things made in clay resist heat and electricity. The insulators on this cable are made from clay.

Clay was used by people
who lived long, long ago.
It is still being used today.
The nose of the space shuttle
is covered with a layer
of tiles made from clay and silica.
The tiles help keep the shuttle cool
as it re-enters the atmosphere.
Who knows how clay
will be used next!

About this book

This book is designed for use in the home, kindergarten and infant school.

Parents can share the book with young children. Its aim is to bring into focus some of the elements of life and living which are all too often taken for granted. To develop fully, all young children need to have their understanding of the world deepened and the language they use to express their ideas extended. This book, and others in the series, takes the everyday things of the child's world and explores them, harnessing curiosity and wonder in a purposeful way.

For those working with young children each book is designed to be used both as a picture book, which explores ideas and concepts and as a starting point to talk and exploration. The pictures have been selected because they are of interest in themselves and also because they include elements which will promote enquiry. Talk can lead to displays of items and pictures collected by children and teacher. Pictures and collages can be made by the children themselves.

Everything in our environment is of interest to the growing child. The purpose of these books is to extend and develop that interest.

Henry Pluckrose